I0788641

BELGIUM 2016 HUMAN RIGHTS REPORT

EXECUTIVE SUMMARY

The Kingdom of Belgium is a parliamentary democracy with a limited constitutional monarchy. The country is a federal state with several levels of government: national; regional (Flanders, Wallonia, and Brussels); language community (Flemish, French, and German); provincial; and local. The Federal Council of Ministers, headed by the prime minister, remains in office as long as it retains the confidence of the lower house (Chamber of Representatives) of the bicameral parliament. Observers considered federal parliamentary elections held in 2014 to be free and fair.

Civilian authorities maintained effective control over the security forces.

The main human rights problem was heightened hostility and discrimination against racial and religious minorities in employment, housing, and societal attitudes. In the aftermath of terrorist attacks in Paris in November 2015 and in Brussels in March, there was an upsurge in reported anti-Islamic incidents across the country, including demonstrations or attempted demonstrations in Brussels, Ghent, and Antwerp. Restrictions on certain forms of religious clothing in public and private sector employment, schools, and public spaces affected Muslim women in particular. Anti-Semitic incidents occurred in schools, the media, and elsewhere in society.

Other human rights problems included a sharp deterioration in prison conditions in May during a strike by prison guards; continued prison overcrowding; domestic violence against women; discrimination against lesbian, gay, bisexual, transgender, and intersex (LGBTI) persons; and trafficking in persons.

Authorities actively prosecuted and punished officials who committed abuses, whether in the security services or elsewhere in government.

Section 1. Respect for the Integrity of the Person, Including Freedom from:

a. Arbitrary Deprivation of Life and other Unlawful or Politically Motivated Killings

There were no reports that the government or its agents committed arbitrary or unlawful killings.

On March 22, terrorists conducted three coordinated suicide bombing attacks in the country: two at the Brussels airport in Zaventem and one at the Maalbeek metro station in central Brussels. The bombings killed 32 civilians and three perpetrators and injured more than 300 persons. Authorities found another bomb during a search of the airport.

b. Disappearance

There were no reports of politically motivated disappearances.

c. Torture and Other Cruel, Inhuman, or Degrading Treatment or Punishment

The law prohibits such practices, and there were no reports that government officials employed them.

Prison and Detention Center Conditions

Prison and detention center conditions met most international standards, although conditions in a number of prisons deteriorated sharply during a strike by prison guards in May.

Physical Conditions: Prison overcrowding remained a problem, despite a steady decrease in the number of inmates, the establishment of new prisons during the year, and the increased use of electronic home monitoring. According to Council of Europe (COE) annual penal statistics, as of January 1, the country's prisons held 12,799 prisoners, including pretrial detainees, while the total capacity of penal institutions was 9,962. As of January 2015, COE statistics indicated there were 13,299 prisoners, including pretrial detainees, in the country's prisons, while the total capacity of penal institutions was 10,135.

According to the media, conditions in a number of prisons deteriorated sharply during a strike by prison guards that began on April 26. On May 19, the COE's commissioner for human rights, Nils Muiznieks, released a statement that he was "extremely concerned" about the situation in a number of the country's prisons "where detainees' living conditions have rapidly deteriorated following a strike carried out by prison guards during the last weeks." Muiznieks noted that, in the most serious cases, "detainees have not been allowed to leave their cells for weeks, have not had access to lawyers or family visits, and have been unable to access medication and use health services." He stated also that sanitary conditions in many cells raised serious concerns due to a lack of regular prisoner access to basic facilities like showers and bathrooms. On May 7 to 9, a delegation from the COE's Committee for the Prevention of Torture (CPT) visited prisons where a large number of staff were absent due to the strike and presented its preliminary observations to the government. The report has not been released to the public.

In 2015 a total of 44 inmates died in prisons, including 16 suicides.

While heating, ventilation, lighting, and sanitary facilities generally were adequate, some older facilities experienced maintenance problems that contributed to poor detention conditions. Medical care was generally adequate, although lengthy wait times to see medical practitioners were sometimes reported. A report from an umbrella organization of nongovernmental organizations (NGOs) active in prisons, however, highlighted the poor level of health, training, and cultural services available to prisoners in francophone prisons, a situation that reportedly jeopardized rehabilitation of prisoners.

Administration: Authorities investigated credible allegations of inhumane conditions and documented these results in a publicly accessible manner. The government investigated and monitored prison and detention center conditions. Surveillance committees tasked with overseeing conditions of imprisonment were active in all the country's prisons.

Independent Monitoring: The federal mediator acts as an ombudsman, allowing any citizen to address problems with prison administration. The federal mediator is an independent entity appointed by the Chamber of Representatives to investigate and resolve problems between citizens and public institutions. Authorities permitted the CPT to visit prisons and detention centers.

d. Arbitrary Arrest or Detention

The law prohibits arbitrary arrest and detention, and the government generally observed these prohibitions.

Role of the Police and Security Apparatus

The federal police are responsible for internal security and nationwide law and order, including migration and border enforcement, and report to the ministers of interior and justice. Civilian authorities maintained effective control over the federal and local police and the armed forces, and the government had effective mechanisms to investigate and punish abuse and corruption.

Arrest Procedures and Treatment of Detainees

Under the constitution an individual may be arrested only while committing a crime or by a judge's order carried out within 24 hours. The law provides detainees the right to prompt judicial determination of the legality of their detention, and authorities generally respected this right. Authorities promptly informed detainees of charges against them and provided access to an attorney (at public expense if necessary). Alternatives to incarceration included conditional release, community service, probation, and electronic monitoring. There was a functioning bail system, and a suspect could be released by meeting other obligations or conditions as determined by the judge. Arrested or detained persons are entitled to challenge in court the legal basis of their detention.

Detainee's Ability to Challenge Lawfulness of Detention before a Court: Detainees have the right to challenge their pretrial detention before a court. They can do so within 24 hours of the notification of detention by the judge, and the court has to rule on the challenge within 15 days. The need for detention is reassessed every three months.

e. Denial of Fair Public Trial

The constitution and law provide for an independent judiciary, and the government generally respected judicial independence.

Trial Procedures

The constitution provides for the right to a fair public trial, and an independent judiciary generally enforced this right. Defendants are presumed innocent and have the right to be informed promptly and in detail of the charges against them; to a fair and public trial without delay; to be present at their trial; to communicate with an attorney of choice; to have adequate time and facilities to prepare defense; free interpretation as necessary from the moment charged through all appeals; to access government-held evidence; to confront witnesses against them and present witnesses and evidence; not to be compelled to testify or confess guilt; and to appeal. The law extends these rights to all citizens.

The law gives domestic courts jurisdiction over war crimes and crimes against humanity that occurred outside the country when the victim or perpetrator was a citizen or legal resident of the country.

Political Prisoners and Detainees

There were no reports of political prisoners or detainees.

Civil Judicial Procedures and Remedies

Individuals and organizations could seek civil remedies for human rights violations through the courts and appeal national-level court decisions to the European Court of Human Rights (ECHR).

f. Arbitrary or Unlawful Interference with Privacy, Family, Home, or Correspondence

The constitution and legal code prohibit such actions, and there were no reports that the government failed to respect these prohibitions.

Section 2. Respect for Civil Liberties, Including:

a. Freedom of Speech and Press

The constitution and law provide for freedom of speech and press, and the government generally respected these rights. An independent press, an effective judiciary, and a functioning democratic political system combined to promote freedom of speech and press.

Freedom of Speech and Expression: Holocaust denial, defamation, sexist remarks and attitudes that target a specific individual, and incitement to hatred are criminal offenses punishable by a minimum of eight days (for Holocaust denial) or one month (incitement to hatred and sexist remarks/attitudes) and up to one year in prison and fines, plus a possible revocation of the right to vote or run for public office. If the incitement to hatred was based on racism or xenophobia, the case would be tried in the regular courts. If, however, the incitement stemmed from other motives, including homophobia or religious bias, a longer and more costly trial by jury generally would be required. The government prosecuted and courts convicted persons under these laws.

In November 2015 a Liege court sentenced French stand-up comedian Dieudonne to two months of prison and a 9,000 euro ($9,900) fine for incitement to hatred, anti-Semitic and discriminatory statements, and Holocaust denial. Dieudonne made the statements during a 2012 one-man show he held in Liege. Police attended and recorded the show. Dieudonne appealed the ruling.

Press and Media Freedoms: The prohibition of Holocaust denial, defamation, sexist remarks and attitudes that target a specific individual, and incitement to hatred apply to the print and broadcast media, the publication of books, and online newspapers and journals.

Internet Freedom

The government did not restrict or disrupt access to the internet or censor online content, and there were no credible reports that the government monitored private online communications without appropriate legal authority. According to estimates compiled by the International Telecommunication Union, approximately 85 percent of the population had access to the internet in 2015.

Academic Freedom and Cultural Events

There were no government restrictions on academic freedom or cultural events.

b. Freedom of Peaceful Assembly and Association

The constitution and law provide for the freedoms of assembly and association, and the government generally respected these rights.

c. Freedom of Religion

See the Department of State's *International Religious Freedom Report* at www.state.gov/religiousfreedomreport/.

d. Freedom of Movement, Internally Displaced Persons, Protection of Refugees, and Stateless Persons

The constitution and the law provide for freedom of internal movement, foreign travel, emigration, and repatriation, and the government generally respected these rights.

The government cooperated with the Office of the UN High Commissioner for Refugees (UNHCR) and other humanitarian organizations in providing protection and assistance to refugees, asylum seekers, stateless persons, or other persons of concern.

Protection of Refugees

Access to Asylum: The law provides for the granting of asylum or refugee status, and the government has established a system for providing protection to refugees, including specific subsidiary protection that goes beyond asylum criteria established by the 1951 Convention relating to the Treatment of Refugees and its 1967 protocol.

Safe Country of Origin/Transit: The country denied asylum to asylum seekers who arrived from a safe country of origin or transit, pursuant to the EU's Dublin III Regulation. Following an ECHR ruling, authorities ceased transferring asylum seekers to Greece if it was the first EU country the asylum seeker entered.

Durable Solutions: The country accepted refugees through UNHCR, including persons located in Italy and Greece, under the EU Emergency Relocation Mechanism. On September 22, one year after the EU agreement to spread refugees across EU countries to support Greece and Italy, Belgium had created 230 spaces for refugees and had effectively resettled 119.

The government facilitated local integration through language and other courses, counseling assistance, and the provision of most of the welfare benefits that other legal residents receive. The country also conducted a voluntary return program for migrants in cooperation with the International Organization for Migration.

Temporary Protection: The country provides temporary protection to individuals who do not satisfy the legal criteria for refugee status but who cannot return to their country of origin due to a real risk of serious harm. Under EU guidelines, individuals granted temporary protection ("subsidiary protection") are entitled to temporary residence permits, travel documents, access to employment, and equal access to health care and housing. In 2015 authorities granted temporary protection to 1,365 persons. For the first half of the year, authorities granted temporary protection to 1,886 persons.

Stateless Persons

According to UNHCR, at the end of 2015, there were 5,776 persons in the country who fell under UNHCR's statelessness mandate. The country does not have a specific legal framework for the protection of stateless persons, and there are no specific procedural rules to determine who is stateless. As a result, authorities applied general texts of laws, such as the judicial code or the General Law on the Foreigners, to find the basis for a statelessness determination in order that the rights of stateless persons were respected on the country's territory. In these general regulations, a person who wants to be qualified as a "stateless" has to file an application before the Tribunal of First Instance, of which there are two.

Section 3. Freedom to Participate in the Political Process

The constitution provides citizens the ability to choose their government in free and fair periodic elections held by secret ballot and based on universal and equal suffrage. Voting in all elections is compulsory; failure to vote is punishable by a nominal fine.

Elections and Political Participation

Recent Elections: Federal elections held in 2014 were considered free and fair.

Participation of Women and Minorities: No laws limit the participation of women and members of minorities in the political process, and women and minorities did participate.

Section 4. Corruption and Lack of Transparency in Government

The law provides criminal penalties for official corruption, and the government generally implemented the law effectively. There were isolated reports of government corruption.

Corruption: In February the media reported an international study had estimated that corruption in public works amounted to approximately 4 billion euros ($4.4 billion) annually. The Office to Combat Corruption of the federal police publicly confirmed the accuracy of the estimate.

Financial Disclosure: The law does not require elected officials to disclose their income or revenue, but they must report if they serve on any board of directors, regardless of whether in a paid or unpaid capacity.

<u>Public Access to Information</u>: With some exceptions, such as material involving national security, the law provides public access to government information. The government effectively implemented the law.

Section 5. Governmental Attitude Regarding International and Nongovernmental Investigation of Alleged Violations of Human Rights

Various domestic and international human rights groups operated without government restriction and were free to investigate and publish their findings on human rights cases. Government officials generally were cooperative and responsive to their views.

<u>Government Human Rights Bodies</u>: Federal and regional government ombudsmen monitored and published reports on the workings of agencies under their respective jurisdictions. The Interfederal Center for Equal Opportunities (Unia) is responsible for promoting equal opportunity and combatting discrimination and exclusion at any level (federal, regional, provincial, or local). The center enjoyed a high level of public trust, was independent in its functioning, and was well financed by the government.

Section 6. Discrimination, Societal Abuses, and Trafficking in Persons

Women

<u>Rape and Domestic Violence</u>: Rape, including spousal rape, is illegal, and the government prosecuted such cases. A convicted rapist may receive 10 to 30 years in prison, depending on factors such as the age of the victim, the difference in age between the offender and the victim, their relationship, and the use or absence of violence during the crime.

The law prohibits domestic violence and provides for fines and incarceration. Legal sanctions for domestic violence are based on the sanctions for physical violence against a third person; the latter range from eight days to 20 years in prison, depending on the means and consequences of the violence. In case of domestic violence, these sanctions are doubled. The law lists several aggravating circumstances, such as violence against the partner and the weakness of the partner (due to age, pregnancy, illness, or handicap.) A number of government-supported shelters and telephone helplines were available across the country for victims of domestic abuse. In addition to providing lodging, many shelters assisted in legal matters, job placement, and psychological counseling to both partners.

<u>Female Genital Mutilation/Cutting (FGM/C)</u>: The law prohibits FGM/C for women and girls. Reported cases were primarily filed by recent immigrants or asylum seekers. Since 2014 two hospitals, in Ghent and Brussels, were reference hospitals for FGM/C victims. There were no new cases reported in 2015, but a recent study estimated that, as of the end of 2012, there were 48,092 women or girls in Belgium who had arrived from a country where FGM/C was practiced. The study estimated that 13,112 individuals were likely excised, while 4,084 were deemed "at risk" of the practice.

The number of requests for asylum in the country based on FGM/C risk declined slightly, from 701 in 2014 to 609 in 2015. Parents often filed requests on behalf of their children. When asylum was granted, authorities followed up to ensure that FGM/C did not take place by having a parent sign a declaration and by requesting a medical certificate each year. Criminal sanctions apply to persons convicted of FGM/C.

<u>Sexual Harassment</u>: The law aims to prevent violence and harassment at work, obliging companies to set up internal procedures to handle employee complaints. Sexist remarks and attitudes targeting a specific individual are illegal; fines for violations range from 50 to 1,000 euros ($55 to $1,100). Reliable statistics on sexual harassment were not easily available, since formal complaints may be filed with various entities. The government generally enforced antiharassment laws. Although there was not a national campaign to fight sexual harassment, politicians and organizations such as the Federal Institute for the Equality of Men and Women worked to raise awareness of the problem.

<u>Reproductive Rights</u>: The constitution includes the right of couples and individuals to decide the number, spacing, and timing of their children; manage their reproductive health; and have the information and means to do so, free from discrimination, coercion, or violence. According to the UN Population Division, 67 percent of women and girls between the ages of 15 and 49 were estimated to have used a modern method of contraception in 2015.

<u>Discrimination</u>: Women have the same legal rights as men, including rights under family, personal status, labor, property, nationality, and inheritance laws. The law requires equal pay for equal work and prohibits discrimination on the grounds of gender, pregnancy, or motherhood as well as sexual intimidation in labor relations and in access to goods, services, social welfare, and health care.

Children

Birth Registration: The government registered all live births immediately. Citizenship is conferred on a child through a parent's (or the parents') Belgian citizenship.

Child Abuse: In 2015 the federal police registered 1,477 complaints of child abandonment, 310 of neglect, 132 of food deprivation, and 3,997 involving physical, sexual, psychological, or other child abuse within the family. The government continued to prosecute cases of child abuse and to punish those convicted. The NGO Child Focus reported handling 1,840 missing child and child abuse cases in 2015.

Early and Forced Marriage: The law provides that both (consenting) partners must be at least 18 years old to marry.

Female Genital Mutilation/Cutting (FGM/C): See information for girls under 18 years of age in the women's section above.

Sexual Exploitation of Children: The law prohibits sexual exploitation, abduction, and trafficking and includes severe penalties for child pornography and possession of pedophilic materials. Authorities enforced the law. The penalties for producing and disseminating child pornography range from five to 15 years' imprisonment and from one month to one year in prison for possessing such material. The law permits the prosecution of residents who commit such crimes while abroad. The law also provides that criminals convicted of child sexual abuse must receive specialized treatment before they can be paroled and must continue counseling and treatment after their release from prison.

According to official figures, the federal police investigated 769 child pornography cases in 2015. Belgian girls and foreign children were subjected to sex trafficking within the country.

The minimum age for consensual sex is 16. Statutory rape carries penalties of imprisonment for 15 to 20 years. If the victim is under 10 years of age, imprisonment increases to 20 to 30 years.

Displaced Children: According to the Belgian Office of Foreigners, 901 unaccompanied minors filed asylum claims as minors between January and June. Authorities provided them adequate housing and services.

<u>International Child Abductions</u>: The country is a party to the 1980 Hague Convention on the Civil Aspects of International Child Abduction. See the Department of State's *Annual Report on International Parental Child Abduction* at travel.state.gov/content/childabduction/en/legal/compliance.html.

Anti-Semitism

The country's Jewish community was estimated at 40,000 persons. There were 570 reports of anti-Semitic acts in 2015. Anti-Semitic acts included some physical attacks but consisted mainly of verbal harassment of Jews and vandalism of Jewish property. Online hate speech continued to be a problem. Jewish groups reported anti-Semitic statements and attitudes in the media and in schools, especially but not exclusively related to the government of Israel and the Holocaust. In one example, the mother of a 12-year-old boy filed a police complaint in June alleging anti-Semitic bullying at a school in the Brussels suburbs, including subjecting him to taunts referencing the Holocaust.

The law prohibits public statements that incite national, racial, or religious hatred, including denial of the Holocaust. The government prosecuted and convicted individuals under this law (see section 2.a.). The government also provided enhanced security at Jewish schools and places of worship.

The Liege court was examining a Holocaust denial case in a francophone school. According to several students, a teacher reportedly mocked Hitler and denied the existence of concentration camps, claiming that the war was not Hitler's but the Jews' fault. He reportedly also said that the number of Jews who died during the war was not as high as the number of persons killed by Americans in Vietnam. A Verviers court sentenced the teacher in December 2015 to one month in prison (suspended sentence) and a 900 euro ($990) fine. The teacher appealed the ruling.

Trafficking in Persons

See the Department of State's *Trafficking in Persons Report* at www.state.gov/j/tip/rls/tiprpt/.

Persons with Disabilities

The law prohibits discrimination against persons with physical, sensory, intellectual, and mental disabilities in employment, education, transportation, access to health care, the judicial system, and the provision of other state services. The government generally enforced the provisions. The Interfederal Center for Equal Opportunities (Unia) received 750 complaints in 2015 (which resulted in 384 effective cases), most related to employment and concerned access to private and public buildings and services, including public transport and access to banks, bars, restaurants, and amusement parks.

While the government mandated that public buildings erected after 1970 must be accessible to such persons, many older buildings were still inaccessible. Although the law requires that inmates with disabilities receive adequate treatment in separate, appropriate facilities, there were approximately 1,000 inmates with disabilities in prisons in spite of the law. The city of Brussels continued construction of accessibility measures on public transportation.

National/Racial/Ethnic Minorities

Ethnic minorities continued to experience discrimination in access to housing, education, and employment.

Government efforts to address such problems included internal training of officials and police officers and enforcement of laws prohibiting such discrimination. Laws and traditions permitting companies and individuals to discriminate on the basis of outward displays of religious belief disproportionately affected women of Moroccan and Turkish ethnic origin.

In 2015 approximately 15 percent of the allegations of discrimination received by Unia were based on physical disabilities. Discriminatory acts primarily took place over the internet, at work, or when individuals attempted to gain access to various public and private services, such as banking and restaurants.

Observers noted that racial discrimination often took the form of religious discrimination or occurred under the guise of practices that ostensibly limited the influence of religion in public life, but that effectively restricted the access of Muslims to employment, housing, and educational opportunities. Discrimination against women who wore a headscarf was common in the labor market. Companies commonly cited policies of "neutrality" with regard to religious belief in justifying such discrimination, although this defense was challenged in courts. The law also prohibits the wearing of a full-face veil (niqab) in public places; the provision affected very few women, compared to employment discrimination experienced by women wearing a headscarf. Authorities may punish persons who discriminate on the basis of ethnic origin with a fine of up to 137.50 euros ($151) and a jail sentence of up to seven days.

There were reports of discrimination against persons of African and Middle Eastern ancestry. For example, a 2015 socioeconomic monitoring report from Unia and the Ministry of Employment noted substantial differences in the employment rates for European Belgians (74.2 percent), Belgo-Moroccans (42.9 percent), and Belgo-Turks (43.3 percent).

Acts of Violence, Discrimination, and Other Abuses Based on Sexual Orientation and Gender Identity

The country has a well-developed legal structure for the protection of LGBTI rights, which are included in the country's antidiscrimination laws. Despite some progress, the underreporting of crimes against the LGBTI community remained a problem.

LGBTI persons from immigrant communities reported social discrimination within those communities. The government supported NGOs working to overcome the problem.

The law provides adequate protections for transgender persons but not for the larger transgender community. It requires a lengthy procedure, including psychiatric diagnosis and physical adaptation of the new gender (including surgery and hormones), before allowing persons to change their gender legally.

During the year the government, in cooperation with the regional entities, implemented an antihomophobia action plan. The plan imposes requirements on government entities involved in family matters, housing, and asylum and migration and calls for awareness campaigns to combat homophobic stereotypes in schools, youth movements, places of work, and the sports community.

Other Societal Violence or Discrimination

In the aftermath of the November 2015 terrorist attacks in Paris and the March bombing attacks in Brussels, there was an upsurge in anti-Islamic incidents across the country, including demonstrations and attempted demonstrations against Islam in Brussels, Ghent, and Antwerp that were attended by hundreds of protesters. There were reports of individual cases of violence directed against Muslims.

In July a petition was circulated in the Brussels municipality of Anderlecht calling on residents to urge Muslims to "go back home" and urging Catholics to set a mosque to a fire. An investigation into the petition was ongoing.

Restrictions on Islamic clothing in public and private sector employment, schools, and public spaces affected Muslim women in particular. In August a school in the Uccle municipality of Brussels forbade two veiled students from taking an examination but relented and allowed them to do so later the same day. The school had earlier changed its regulations to prohibit headscarves as of September 1. The Francophone minister for adult education expressed disappointment over the case and called on the school to provide a solid justification for the ban (schools are free to adopt such a ban, but the ban is required to be justified).

Unia received complaints of discrimination based on physical characteristics, political orientation, social origin, or status. Each of these categories accounted for approximately 3 percent of the total number of complaints filed. In 2015 the center received no notifications involving possible discrimination against persons with HIV/AIDS but opened three HIV/AIDS-related cases.

Section 7. Worker Rights

a. Freedom of Association and the Right to Collective Bargaining

For companies with more than 50 employees, the law provides workers the right to form and join independent unions of their choice without previous authorization or excessive requirements, conduct legal strikes, and bargain collectively. Workers exercised these rights, and citizen and noncitizen workers enjoyed the same rights. Work council elections are mandatory in enterprises employing more than 100 employees, and safety and health committee elections are mandatory in companies employing more than 50 employees. These elections took place in May without incident. Employers sometimes used judicial recourse against associations attempting to prevent workers who did not want to strike from entering the employer's premises.

The law provides for the right to strike for all public and private workers except the military. The law prohibits antiunion discrimination and employer interference in union functions, and the government protected this right. Trade union representatives cannot be fired for performing their duties and are protected against being fined by their employers; they are also entitled to regular severance payments. An employee can request reinstatement if he or she was fired illegally, and employers may be fined for failure to comply. Trade unions had the resources necessary to bring cases to court and could organize labor strikes if necessary. The fine for terminating a trade union representative or a nonelected candidate is the equivalent of the salary due the employee until the end of his or her mandate as trade union representative, up to four years.

The government generally enforced applicable laws. Resources, inspections, and remediation were adequate. Penalties were generally not sufficient to deter violations as employers often paid fines rather than reinstate workers fired for union activity. At the same time, fines on workers for strike or collective bargaining actions often resulted in breaking strike movements. Administrative or judicial procedures related to trade unions were not longer than other court cases.

Freedom of association and the right to bargain collectively were inconsistently respected by employers. Worker organizations were generally free to function outside of government control. Unions complained that judicial intervention in collective disputes undermined collective bargaining rights.

b. Prohibition of Forced or Compulsory Labor

The law prohibits all forms of forced or compulsory labor, but such practices occurred. The government effectively enforced the law; resources, inspections, and remediation efforts were adequate. Legal penalties include a maximum prison sentence of 20 years and were sufficient to deter violations.

Women from Eastern Europe, sub-Saharan Africa, and Asia were subjected to sexual exploitation. Forced and compulsory labor included male victims forced to work in restaurants, bars, sweatshops, agriculture, construction, cleaning, and retail sites. Foreign victims were subjected to forced domestic service. Forced begging continued, particularly in the Romani community.

Also see the Department of State's *Trafficking in Persons Report* at www.state.gov/j/tip/rls/tiprpt/.

c. Prohibition of Child Labor and Minimum Age for Employment

The minimum age of employment is 15. Persons between the ages of 15 and 18 may participate in part-time work/study programs and work full time during school vacations. The Ministry of Employment regulated industries that employ juvenile workers to ensure that labor laws were followed; it occasionally granted waivers for children temporarily employed by modeling agencies and in the entertainment business. Waivers were granted on a short-term basis and for a clearly defined performance or purpose that had to be listed in the law as an acceptable activity. The law clearly defines, according to the age of the child, the amount of time that may be worked daily and the frequency of performance. A child's earnings must be paid to a bank account under the name of the child, and the money is inaccessible until the child reaches 18 years of age.

There are laws and policies to protect children from exploitation in the workplace. The government generally enforced these laws with adequate resources, inspections, and penalties, although such practices reportedly occurred. Persons found in violation of child labor laws could face a prison sentence ranging from six months to three years, as well as administrative fines.

d. Discrimination With Respect to Employment and Occupation

Labor laws and regulations related to employment or occupation prohibit discrimination based on race, sex, gender, disability, language, sexual orientation and/or gender identity, HIV-positive status or other communicable diseases, or social status. The government effectively enforced these laws and regulations. The law continued to permit companies to prohibit outward displays of religious affiliation, including headscarves (see section 6).

Employers discriminated in employment and occupation against women, persons with disabilities, and members of certain minorities as well as against internal and foreign migrant workers. The government took legal action based on antidiscrimination laws. The Interfederal Center for Equal Opportunities (Unia) also facilitated arbitration or other settlements in some cases of discrimination. Such settlements could involve monetary payments, community service, or other demands imposed on the offender.

The Employment and Labor Relations Federal Public Service generally enforced regulations effectively. Trade unions or media sometimes escalated cases, and Unia often took a position or acted as a go-between to find solutions or to support alleged victims in the courts.

The Federal Institute for the Equality of Men and Women is responsible for promoting gender equality and may initiate lawsuits if it discovers violations of equality laws. Most complaints received during the year were work-related and most concerned the termination of employment contracts due to pregnancy.

Economic discrimination against women continued. In 2015 the institute released a survey (based on 2013 data) indicating that women were paid at an hourly rate that was 8 percent less than their male colleagues. This represented an annual gap of 21 percent, taking into account part-time work. The law requires that one-third of the board members of publicly traded companies, but not private ones, be women.

The law requires companies with at least 50 employees to provide a clear overview of their compensation plans, a detailed breakdown by gender of their wages and fringe benefits, a gender-neutral classification of functions, and the possibility of appointing a mediator to address and follow up on gender-related problems.

e. Acceptable Conditions of Work

Since January 2015 the monthly national minimum wage has been 1,501.82 euros ($1,650) for workers who were 18 years of age; 1,541.67 euros ($1,700) for workers who were 19 1/2 years of age with six months of service; and 1,559.38 euros ($1,720) for workers who were 20 years of age with one year of service.

The standard workweek is 38 hours, and workers are entitled to four weeks of annual leave. Departure from these norms can occur under a collective bargaining agreement, but work may not exceed 11 hours per day or 50 hours per week. An 11-hour rest period is required between work periods. Overtime is paid at a time-and-a-half premium Monday through Saturday and at double time on Sundays. The Ministry of Labor and the labor courts effectively enforced these laws and regulations. The law forbids or limits excessive overtime. Without specific authorization, an employee may not work more than 65 hours of overtime during any one quarter.

The Employment and Labor Relations Federal Public Service generally enforced regulations effectively. Inspectors from both the Ministry of Labor and the Ministry of Social Security enforced labor regulations. These ministries jointly worked to ensure that standards were effectively enforced in all sectors, including the informal sector, and that wages and working conditions were consistent with collective bargaining agreements.

A specialized governmental department created to fight the informal economy conducted 13,345 investigations in 2015, mainly in the construction, restaurant/hotel, and cleaning sectors. The department found 7,719 infractions, including instances of unregistered businesses or workers, documentation of incorrect schedules, or unregistered foreign workers. Authorities may fine employers for poor working conditions but may also treat them as cases of trafficking in persons. Fines may range from administrative to criminal sanctions depending on a range of factors, including the nature of the infraction, its consequences, and the length of time the infraction occurred.

Workers may remove themselves from situations that endanger health or safety without jeopardy to their employment. The Employment and Labor Relations Federal Public Service protected employees in this situation.

NOTES